How To Style Modestly And Rule Your World

by

Musarrat Binti Salam

Copyright © 2019

Table of Contents

Introduction

Being bold and confident in human society is the best thing that can happen to any person and—at the same time—one of the most difficult things. It takes a high level of understanding and acceptance of individualism for one to come to terms with the fact that trying too hard to please everybody even in one's personal life is a high way to an early grave.

There has never been a time in history when the woman is allowed to express herself the way she wants without being judged and told what to do by every Tom, Dick, and Harry. She is the center of attraction in every moral discussion and the specimen for every self-oppressing societal norm.

The fashion industry is the number one place where lack of freedom for the woman to express herself is most predominant. She is not allowed to wear what she wants but rather what society wants her to wear; her body is hardly her body, but *our* body as a society since the decision on what to wear and how to wear them is made for her collectively by society. This has led to fashion meaning different things to different women overtime, and most times things totally unconnected with the beauty of fashion as art.

There has always been a religious or cultural undertone to women's fashion, which has acted as tools to dictate to the woman what to wear. As a result, with the rise of feminism, many women are pushing aside the dictates of society even in fashion and are all about self-expression. This is quite good, but the sad thing about it, is that women all seem to be moving in one direction of baring their bodies to public view as a way of proving that they own their bodies and can do with it as they please.

It seems that the trademark of the average independent woman who is free from the bondage of society is to go almost unclad in public. This has been the trend. Any time a woman proclaims her independence, she is at the same time declaring war on modest clothing. It is this reoccurrence that birthed our topic for discussion in this book.

There is a need for us to change the narrative of modest fashion. We need to start seeing it as a beautiful way of respecting our bodies, which does not necessarily stifle our individual tastes. You do not need to be a Muslim woman before you can dress modestly and you can still be stylish and fashionable even in modest apparels. The twenty-first-century fashion industry is beginning to make room for modest fashion and this change in the right direction has come to stay.

For anything we do in life to be effective, we always need to strike a balance and go for moderation. And what better way is there to be moderate in our clothing styles than to embrace modest fashion. In this book, we are going to look at all the sides there are to modest fashion, show you why you should explore the modest side of fashion if you are interested in being confident as a woman and empowered to rule your world.

Let's dig in.

Chapter One

What is Modest Fashion: A Throwback

I mentioned in the introductory chapter that women are always being told what to do with their bodies and the kind of clothes they should wear. Meanwhile, I am going ahead to try to encourage you to embrace modern fashion. Does it not seem like I am doing the same thing I have rightly accused society of doing—trying to tell you the kind of clothes to wear? That would have been true if there are specific sets of clothes that go by the name modest fashion.

So what is modern fashion? The first thing that comes to the mind of the average woman when modest fashion is mentioned is the style of clothing of Muslim women. Yes, that is modest fashion, about the height of it; but you do not necessarily need to wear the hijab before you can dress modestly. Any woman, irrespective of religion or personality, can dress modestly. The point is not for every woman to have a uniform look, but for us to cover up sensitive parts of our body for many reasons we shall look into later.

Modest fashion recently started making headlines in fashion magazines and there is now what we can call the global modest fashion market; but there is a journey that transcends this recent development. Modest fashion has been around all the while and we will take a look back into a bit of history.

There have always been women who dress modestly; and while many of them are for cultural or religious reasons, some dress modestly because of the position of authority they occupy in society and they want to be the kind of women younger girls would look up to.

They want to be role models. Therefore, modest dressing has always been a thing.

But its emergence into mainstream fashion began in the early years of the twenty-first century when the big names in fashion design began to take interest in the modest side to fashion. Though initially inspired by the religious aspect to it, as it was mostly about designs that met the taste of Muslim women, designers have discovered a huge market for modest fashion and the fact that other women are beginning to embrace it for aesthetic purposes as well has made the market to keep expanding.

The internet and social media have also been fuel to the fire of modest fashion. Some women, especially young women, who would have loved to dress modestly but didn't for fear of being called old fashioned are beginning to get inspiration from the bold women who dress modestly and have a huge following on social channels.

It is fast becoming more widely accepted and more women are beginning to embrace the modest side of themselves. What is most exciting about the entrance of modest fashion into mainstream fashion is that it is not a fad. It has come to stay. I know this because it has taken a slow and steady approach and gradually come to this point.

Chapter Two

There is More to Fashion than Meets the Eye

Miuccia Prada says, "What you wear is how you present yourself to the world, especially today, when human contacts are so quick. Fashion is instant language." This is a glaring truth. Clothes mean a lot more to us than just what we put on our bodies. When you see a beautiful dress on that lady, to you, it may be just a beautiful dress. But, to her, it may mean more than that; she may even have some kind of philosophy around it. let's look at some of the meanings fashion has to different people.

An Item for Covering: there are some people who do not attach much meaning to the idea of fashion. To them, clothes are just clothes and nothing more.

They do not understand why other people spend so much money, time, and effort on clothes. This category of people is very rare. You can hardly meet anyone who does not have some sort of attachment to the clothes they wear. There is hardly anyone who does not take their time to select the kind of things they put on their body. That notwithstanding, there are still people who wear clothes just for the sake of wearing clothes.

Beauty: Our natural bodies may not be as beautiful as they usually are when they are covered in beautiful dresses. Women especially see fashion as a tool for beautifying themselves. No matter your body type and the size you came in, there are clothes that will flatter your body and even make other women admire you. For many women out there, they are only as beautiful as the kind of clothes they wear. This category of women spends a lot of money and time picking beautiful dresses that will make them feel good about themselves. For them, fashion is all about how beautiful they feel in a dress.

Confidence Booster: while fashion means beauty to some women, for some others, it means confidence. Do you have some dresses that when you wear them, you feel so sure about yourself and the things you can do? Mind you, these are just items of clothing but they have the power to boost your confidence. when you are going for an interview or a first date, you usually pick the kind of clothes that will make you feel comfortable and confident at the same time. Yes, we always wear clothes and the clothes we wear can become the channel through which we grow our self-confidence.

An Identity: some women wear only some particular kind of clothes, a kind of signature. This is common among entertainers. The clothes they wear most often become what people know them for. They become what people remember when they think about them. This is one of the things that can be done with fashion.

Creativity: Like music, movies and the other arts, fashion is a full-blown form of artistic expression. This is mostly for designers who are the reason fashion keeps evolving. But individuals also find fashion as a means of expressing their creativity through what they wear and how they wear it.

The colors, the design, the materials—they all mean more than what is seen. The combination of these three properties births beautiful apparels that take up the body of women as a medium of expression. There is a deep aesthetic to fashion.

Escapism: some other women use fashion as a tool for escape. This is usually the case when they are not getting the kind of life they want. So, they wear dresses that negate their reality as a form of defiance to that reality. Clothing to them is some kind of performance. For this category of women, there is some kind of obsession with fashion. They devote time and money into what they wear.

Cultural Implications: I have mentioned earlier, albeit briefly, that fashion for some women have cultural undertones. Some women wear clothes that express their world view, which is grounded in the culture that formed their minds and their thinking patterns. Consequently, as fashion keeps evolving from one generation to the next, these cultural undertones find their way into trends.

Emotional Implications: Women are very emotional beings. Many of us get attached to things easily and develop sentiments over things around us. Shiona Turini, a freelance stylist and fashion consultant, when interviewed by Leandra Medine, has this to say about fashion:

Fashion ties us to moments of our existence. It adds to the elements of our emotional and physical sensories by being a literal fabric and thread in our lives. I'll never forget the feeling of saving enough money to buy a green Benetton rugby shirt or the yellow dress with brown pom-poms that I had when I was four. Think about how emotionally tied you become to a wardrobe in a film—to me, that is the point of fashion: to help connect and mark time.

Whatever fashion may mean to you is valid. It is only important that we acknowledge that it means a whole lot of other things to other people as well. When we begin to see fashion holistically, we can approach it better and make it work for us.

Chapter Three

Fashion as a Medium of self-expression

When you were a little girl, your parents probably picked the clothes you wore and made all the choices for you, including fashion choices. Maybe for them, it wasn't about fashion; it was just about what would cover you up according to the weather at any point in time. So, you or what you wanted never came to play in the kind of outfits you wore.

But one mark of adulthood is that we begin to make our own decisions and take responsibility for our actions. What most women do once they become adults is to change their wardrobes and wear only the things they like to wear, the kind of things that define them and make meaning to them. While some choose their clothing according to trend, others have a steady pattern they follow when it comes to what they wear. That brings us to the difference between fashion and style.

We've been using fashion loosely all this while to mean clothing in general and all that has to do with picking the kind of clothes we wear and we will continue to use it loosely that way as we go on. But there is a difference between the words fashion and style.

Fashion in the strict sense of the word is determined by the fashion designers and expressed through trends. A piece of fashion item that trends today may become old fashioned by this time next year because fashion designers are constantly working to bring more things into the market. So, the hallmark of fashion is change, constant change. There is always instability and you can hold on to a fading trend without coming across to other people as old fashioned.

Style, on the other hand, is you creating your own personal clothing experience from what is available in fashion. When you are for style, you have some kind of things you wear and those you will not wear no matter how widely they trend. Style is stable and expresses individual taste, not a collective fad. Style is stable and only gets adjusted with new developments in the fashion industry.

Anybody can be a part of fashion and trends. In fact, the average person wants to wear what everyone else is wearing. But a person of style is not moved by changes in fashion. Even if all the women in the world have worn the latest trend but it does not work for her, the woman of style does not even notice. Likewise, the high level of confidence that it takes to get to the level where you close your eyes on what every other woman is wearing is what I want you to achieve because you will need a whole lot of confidence if you are going to practice modest dressing.

Choosing fashion over style does not necessarily mean that you will not wear stuff just because they are fashionable. No. you can wear fashionable items of clothing if they fit into your personal style. In other words, it is not about being fashionable or not, but about being yourself. Iris Apfel says, *"Fashion you can buy, but style you possess. The key to style is learning who you are, which takes years. There is no how-to road map to style. It's about self-expression and, above all, attitude."* And that sums it all up. Clothes become a medium of self-expression to you when you have a personal style that portrays your individual identity.

Chapter Four

Styling with Modest Fashion

We've been talking about how clothing means different things to different people and how fashion, in the strict sense of the word, is different from style. The question is, what have all these got to do with our main topic of consideration here, which is modern fashion? I know you may have this question going on in your mind and the answer is that we need a proper foundation before we can delve into the main deal for proper understanding.

The beauty of modest dressing is that you can dress modestly no matter what your personal style may be. It is all about covering up your body. When you have a personal style that does not bend to suit into every trend in the fashion industry, it becomes easier for you to maintain modesty in your dressing. It is no news that nudity sells today faster than any other commodity which is why we keep having trends that are too revealing for women.

The truth is that designers will keep designing and pushing into the market things that appeal to the common consumer. And you have what it takes to shun whatever it is that is trending and go for items that show some regard for your body. Never allow what you see in the market or on other women determine what you do.

You are different, confident, and a queen in the kingdom of your life. You shouldn't dance to the tune of your immediate surrounding when it comes to fashion and anything else, as a matter of fact. The test of true confidence is when you are able to be yourself even when everyone else expects you to be something else. You need some defiance, the kind of defiance which is exemplified in the act of having a personal style. Every time society wants to win you over with a new item on their fashion trend that does not conform to your personal style, you push them down, rise above them, and show forth your style like light that cannot be hidden.

Modest dressing and having a personal style work side by side and can only be done by women who believe that they are complete all by themselves.

Chapter Five

Be Unapologetically you in Style

Before you make up your mind to be a person of style and have your own unique style, you should have come to terms with the fact that people are not going to mind their business. They will try to tell you what to wear and how you should wear it. This is the major reason the average woman out there easily blends into fashion trends and loses her individuality.

Society is obsessed with what women wear. If you dress modestly, you will be termed old fashioned; if you dress to kill, you will still be labeled negatively. If this is the case, what then should a woman do? Simple: shun society and do you. You are all the approval and validation that you need. Nobody can rule your life unless you give them the power to control you. Never forget this.

People will always try to tell you what to do, but once you stand up for yourself and ignore them, they will back away or at least say whatever they want to say from a distance and give you the respect you deserve. When you discover your style, own it; own it with pride. This is your only shot at life and you need to be brave enough to live it to the fullest in spite of anyone who will try to convince you to the contrary.

Becoming bold enough to bask in your personal style is actually not as easy as it may sound. It takes some gradual process of deliberate self-discovery and acceptance. Here are very important steps you should take I you want to be unapologetically yourself while owning your own style in modest fashion.

Discover what works for you: the first thing you need to do is to understand your body type and know what works for you. Many women put on any item of clothing for the singular reason that it is trending. They do not care about whether it suits their body type or not; and that is wrong thinking in fashion. You should wear what suits your body and not force your body into anything. If you wear something simply because it is beautiful and trendy even when it does not suit your body type, you will not be as confident as you should.

There is a kind of confidence that wearing the right clothes gives. You will go about your business of the day knowing that you have done the right thing in your appearance. But when you wear an ill-fitting dress, perhaps because it is available, you will keep wondering why people are looking at you, whether they even notice you or not.

Women on the plus size side are mostly guilty of this. Some plus size women try to fit themselves into trending clothes that are obviously for the slender body type. They know that this won't look great on them, but because they do not have the confidence to ignore some trends, they wear these clothes and go out feeling insecure. Please try to discover what works for your body type as a woman. That is the foundation to being confident in modest fashion.

Declutter Your Wardrobe: before you can truly start doing the right thing, you have to get rid of old wrong habits. When it comes to fashion, your old habits can be found in your wardrobe. You need to do a decluttering and take away all the clothes that should not be there. This is perhaps not going to be easy because you must have been used to those clothing items.

Well, changing into a new lifestyle is never easy, you just have to be brave enough to do it. And when you do, you will start reaping the benefits. So, after discovering the kind of clothing that works for you, give out all the ones in your wardrobe that do not work. Get rid of the old ones, too. Some women wear clothes, especially their favorite clothes, until they are so worn and tired.

You cannot walk confidently if you are wearing an old and tired piece of clothing. So, as you are discarding the items of clothing that do not work for your body type, also discard the ones that are too old to be worn by a beautiful woman like you. You deserve to wear what suits your body.

Have your way around Colors: do you consider color as a factor when you are shopping for clothes? Do you wear anything that fits perfectly whether the color suits you or not? There is also this notion that darker colors are for mature people and bright colors for kids. But that does not make sense. Pick the colors that work for you; but while you are at it, go for variety even within the colors that suit you.

Keep it Tidy: Modest fashion has a lot more to it than just clothes. The accessories and makeup that go with the clothes you wear are all part of it and you should use them in such a way that your confidence will not be deemed. Some women dress modestly but when you look at them, you won't admire modest dressing at all. They do it in a way that depicts some kind of perpetual tiredness. They do not make any effort to tidy up and appear smart. Whatever fashion orientation you have, you should always endeavor to tidy up your appearance.

Keep it Simple: you can never go wrong with simplicity. When you are confused about what to wear, a simple outfit will always come to the rescue. You do not need too many things on your body before you can appear beautiful. The less complicated you look, the more beautiful and appealing you will be. How many colors do you wear on your face every day in the name of makeup? What kind of hairstyle do you carry? What kind of designs do you go for? All these contribute to your overall look which determines whether you will carry yourself boldly or not. Simplicity is classy.When you take note of all these factors and work on them, you would be amazed at the woman you will be seeing in the mirror.

Chapter Six

The Empowered and Confident Woman

If there is just one thing you need to survive in society as a woman, it is the ability to be your own woman. What do I mean by that? Because of the dictates of society, the average woman most likely grew up in an environment that stifles her personality and ensures that she is nothing close to what she wants to be. From your parents dictating to you, to your husband dictating to you, you hardly know what your true self really is.

The worst of them all is that even other people who have no business in your life also try to get themselves involved and tell you what to do with your life. And with the advent of the internet and social media, more people have access to seeing you and telling you what to do with your body.

You need to be empowered and confident before you can boldly live among other men and women and be your own woman. There are many ways you could do this and many steps to take, but our focus here is on modest fashion so we will talk about how you can empower yourself through the kind of things you wear.

We've talked about discovering your own style away from the noise of fashion. Do you know that what eventually enters mainstream fashion are the bold steps some trailblazers in the fashion industry make? It does not matter whether you have seen anyone else dress that way or not. Once you take the bold step and style in your own way, you are taking the lead for others to follow. Many women know this, but only a few act on this knowledge.

We know that when we are bold enough to express your true selves, society will adjust. So, why do we still copy other women? Why do we bend our lives and shrink our personalities just to belong? The answer lies in the fact that many women are not empowered to be themselves. There is deliberate conditioning of the mind that needs to happen to you and you are the only person who can make that happen. You cannot leave your choices in the hands of society and become an empowered woman. The first thing you do to empower yourself is to take the power over your life choices away from society.

It is interesting to note that when we talk about society, we are not talking about an individual or even a group of persons. Society is an idea that that really has no tangible footing over your life unless you give it the power to do that. When you want to do something, say cover up your body instead of going almost unclad, you may have some doubts, especially if you are trying this for the first time. You are most likely going to ask yourself, what will people say? What will your friends say? And, if you are a celebrity, what will your fans say?

Let's begin with "what will people say?" When you ask that question, who does the word "people" refer to? You can agree with me that it refers to nobody in particular—maybe random people in society. But why should you be making your life's decisions based on what people who know little or nothing about you and care absolutely nothing about you think? Does that even begin to make sense? I want you to think about it.

Then you have the "what will my friends say?" question. May I let you know that anybody in your life who is worthy to be called your friend should always respect your decisions whether it suits them or not. That you have friends does not mean that you will live your life based on 'groupthink' or group decision. You are the master of your own life and what your friends should do is just to give you some advice if they think that you are going in the wrong direction. And of course, you are not under any obligation to take all advice especially when it has to do with changing your mind about something that is actually for your own good.

"What will my fans say?" Most celebrities are entrapped in this choking web of what will my fans say? They live for their fans and everything they do is to look good for the camera. They wear all the trending stuff just to feel among and spend money on the things they do not really need just to impress their fans. The entertainment industry is the headquarters of all sorts of indecent dressing. Entertainers who are willing to dress modestly in their personal lives are very few, and this is simply because they want to be what their fans want to see.

However, there is nothing your fans will want to see more than celebrities who are true to themselves. They may react at first but will definitely get used to who you truly are. You should never live to please your fans who will love you only for as long as you are in the limelight. If, unfortunately, you fail, your so-called fans will move on to the next big thing. Now, are these the people you want to consider when you are making personal decisions?

Take your mind off what people around you will say. Be mindful of the fact that there are bullies everywhere ready to bully you if you let them have their way. The more you let them bully you, the more power you give them over your life. What I want you to take away from this chapter is that the primary prerequisite for empowering yourself is to take up courage and be yourself unapologetically.

Chapter Seven

Covering up is Classy

It is normal for women from countries like India and Pakistan to clothe themselves in modest apparels. It is also expected of Muslim women to cover up their bodies with long flowing dresses, the hijab and all. This is understandable because of the cultural and religious significance such clothing style holds for them respectively.

However, modest fashion has a different reaction when it comes to western cultures. Years back, women were meant to dress modestly even in the West because that is what society demands. If you are a woman who loves showing off some flesh, you would be regarded as wayward back then. But the rise of women empowerment began to make for changes even in women's fashion. Fashion is a form of cultural expression, so women began to express themselves through fashion. They began to wear the kind of clothes that society frowned at as a way of expressing defiance over society and proving that they have control over their body.

I want to ask you right now—woman to woman—do you sincerely think that the best way to express control over your body is to bare it all in public? Do you think that the best way to show that you are no longer in the bondage of culture is to do the exact opposite of what culture demands? If this is what you do, it means that you are not totally free from the culture you are fighting against. It still informs your choices and your decisions, albeit in the opposite direction.

An empowered and confident woman lives a wholesome life that is not based on decisions taken because of the goings on in society. She is very secure and does not try to prove anything to anybody. She knows her worth. She knows that her worth as a woman is not tied to what other people think of her. She is decent and clothes herself in modest apparels. When she walks into a room, eyes turn, not to feed on her body, but to admire her personality. That is the definition of class. Modest fashion is indeed classy.

Do you know that the average woman is expected to dress up in revealing outfits? If she is not showing off her thighs, she should be showing off her cleavage, or both. So, while you think you are expressing control over your body by wearing anything you like, the true controllers are the people you are trying to prove yourself to. When you say, "Society, I can bare my body in your face and you cannot do anything about it." you are simply saying that your choice of outfits is dependent on society's expectations, whether for or against it.

There is nothing as classy as a woman who holds her shit together; and her shit here extends to those parts of her body that are supposed to be considered as her private part. You should always leave people guessing what you have covered up there instead of baring everything and leaving nothing to the imagination. A classy woman is enigmatic. You can never fully tell what she is up to and this is reflected in the kind of clothes she puts on her body.

When society expects you to wear in a less modest way, disappoint them and cover up your body and you will win their respect and admiration. This is not about religious or cultural concerns now. Far from it. It is about you owning class and meeting up to it. It is about you being different in a good way.

If you observe strong and confident women out there who have attained global recognition, one thing you will realize that is common among them is that they do not appear in public wearing skimpy dresses. They portray class. That is what I want for you. I want you to attain the level of confidence that will make you wear what your body will thank you for. Your ability to ignore what is trending and wear what is classy is the beginning of your empowerment.

Chapter Eight

The True First Impression

The popular saying is that you do not have a second chance to make a first impression. First impressions truly matter. Though I personally would say that you cannot truly tell the character of a person by the first impression you have of them. You may meet someone for the first time when they are having a bad day. Everybody has the right to have a bad day at least once in a while and even the best of us are vulnerable to this. So, if you meet a really nice person unfortunately on the day they are having a bad day, you will walk away with the wrong impression of them.

But then life is not fair and most times we truly do not have a second chance to correct a wrong first impression. What this means is that you should be at your best at all times, especially when you are meeting someone for the first time. I included at all times because sometimes we meet very important people without planning to meet them at all. The major part of being your best for any occasion is looking your best. That is the true first impression. Before anyone can form an opinion about you, they should see you first. And guess what they see first when they encounter you...your outfit.

Any impression that the person you are meeting for the first time holds about you from what you say during the encounter is a second impression. Do you know why it is very important that you dress modestly as much as you can? It is because you do not know who is watching. I know that modest dressing used to be seen as a very conservative thing to do—it has gone mainstream now, though—there are people who are in charge of what you want but may not give it to you because they have a negative impression about you just because of the way you dress.

Why do we dress modestly to job interviews? Why do we dress modestly for our presentations? Why do we dress modestly when we have an invitation to the White House? Why do we dress modestly when we are meeting very important people? If going about almost unclad is cool, why do we not do it when we are doing very important things in our lives? It is simply because we want to give the right impression. We want people to have a good impression of us. The twenty-first century style of living and working has it that people are always too busy. In some cases, people do not even have the time and patience to listen to you to discover your personality. They go away with what they can make of your physical appearance.

At all times, do your best to dress modestly. It depicts class and confidence. No serious minded person will want to see your body first before encountering your mind. Some may conclude that they do not want to encounter you if their first impression of you was not a good one.

Chapter Nine

Modest Fashion is Current Fashion

Gone are the days when only religion or some cultural obligation make women dress modestly. Gone are the days when only old and middle-aged women dress modestly. You no longer have to be a Muslim woman before you can dress modestly without raising eyebrows.

Modest fashion has entered the mainstream fashion industry and it has come to stay. I am convinced that this development is not a fad because it didn't come with the sudden fire that is typical of new fashion trends. It is more like a revolution and inclusion of modesty into what women wear.

The market for modest fashion has always been very negligible—mostly just for Muslim women. Designers didn't go head-on into modest fashion because most women would readily prefer the opposite of modest fashion. But that is changing now. Designers are beginning to take advantage of the modest fashion market because there are actually women out there who prefer dressing modestly.

DKNY, H&M, Dolce & Gabanna, and even Nike are big fashion labels that have begun to cater to the modest fashion market. H&M has the LTD collection strictly for modest fashion. Muslim models are also making it bold and dressing modestly even for the camera.

Mariah Idrissi, the British model and public speaker who modelled for H&M in 2015 has been of great influence in the modest fashion movement. Halima Aden, the American fashion model, also made it bold to wear her hijab in a pageant and has graced the cover of British Vogue in a hijab.

We know how influential social media is in our time and the modest fashion movement is also leveraging that through the likes of Maria Alia and Dian Pelangi on Instagram and many others across other social channels. It is actually a season for modest fashion and many women are beginning to look in that direction. Bloggers are taking up the niche and retailers are stocking up modest clothing for women.

We are beginning to have modest fashion weeks and women all over the world are seeing another dimension to fashion. So, if your reason for ignoring or avoiding modesty in your appearance is because you think that it is not cool, you can change your mind now because modest fashion is the new cool. You can look up ways to incorporate it into your personal style.

One exciting thing about this trend is that it is so much more than just a trend. It is a revolution that has come to stay. It is not the crazy fashion trend that goes just as fast as it comes. This one has taken years and is patiently penetrating the market.

In a nutshell, modest fashion is not old fashioned. It is current fashion and its currency is the type that will be sustained from generation to generation and championed by women who are confident in themselves. Are you ready?

Chapter Ten

Don't Mask your Insecurities

Every human has an area in their life that they are not proud of, which makes them insecure when they have to deal with it. It is common knowledge that most women are very insecure about their looks. Society is not very accepting of the big body size and having excess fat in your body also has some disastrous health implication, which is the reason chubby people are always trying to shed some fat.

One would have thought that slim women would be very happy with their looks. On the contrary, however, we see slim women battling with one thing or the other about their body. It's either they want bigger butts or they want larger boobs. This is why most women keep looking for artificial things to make up for what they think is lacking in their body.

But there are women who are comfortable in their own skin, women who do not place their self-worth in their looks. These are confident women. The best thing that can happen to any woman is for her to develop a deep sense of confidence in herself. Before you can start appreciating the beauty of modest fashion, you need to appreciate the beauty of your body and understand the way it works in its unique form. You need to stop comparing your body with those of other women; that is the chief killer of confidence. And how can you do this? You can by simply understanding that every woman came in her own unique package and none is necessarily better than the other.

When you see models on the covers of fashion magazines, try not to envy them or crave to be like them. Appreciate their looks and do not compare. You are going to hurt yourself if you try to be like someone else. By the way, the models you compare yourself with dressed up for the camera and took several shots from which the best were selected and put on the cover of the magazine. What you are seeing is a perfected version of what the model truly looks like in real life. So, why would you want to compare your real life with someone else's performance? It sincerely does not make sense.

There is more to fashion than just to cover up your insecurities. If you do not confront your insecurities, they will keep hunting you and you can never become a confident woman. Beauty is beyond the things you wear; it is beyond just what the eyes can see. It is not skin deep. Your personality and your understanding of life around you are great components of your overall beauty matrix. You can only begin to appreciate this dimension of beauty when you take your eyes off the things that do not matter.

Don't get me wrong. It is vital that you take care of your body and look beautiful. But the point is that when looks become the driving force of your life; when you begin to stand before the mirror for hours wearing makeup and can never step out of the house without having makeup on; when you always want to wear what the next girl is wearing, there is a serious problem you should address.

I understand that insecurities are part of life. Any human will always have one thing or the other about themselves that they are not proud of. However, do not try to cover it up. Confront it. If it is something that can be worked on, please, by all means, do work on it and get what you want. If you are overweight, all you need is to be disciplined enough to make the right choices: eat the right things in the right proportions, exercise, and repeat consistently. Then you will watch yourself slide back into the body of your dreams. But if you try to look for a short-cut way around it, you might have that heavy weight for a long time. Stop looking for "Five easy steps to lose weight without exercise or going on a diet". It simply does not exist. There are no easy steps to getting good results. No, life is not that rosy. You might get scammed, waste money, and still remain in the same weight.

Some women are not comfortable with their faces. It's either they do not like the shape of their faces or they simply would prefer a different face. And what do we have? They always smear their faces up in makeup. Makeup is good when it is used to accentuate beauty. You can make up modestly, too. When you apply too many colors on your face such that one would have to take a closer look in order to recognize you, then you are getting it all wrong. The modest way is the simple way and it is always better. If you feel that you are ugly, you need to confront that part of your life. You did not choose the face you came in; none of us did. For that reason, you should try to come to terms with what you have and become comfortable with it. You should love yourself so much that you love every part of your body. When you do, other people will also learn how to love you.

Could it be your skin color? Would you have preferred a different color? The truth is that no one color is superior to others. It is what you carry on the inside that matters. A woman's confidence is not dependent on her physical features. You are worth more than your body type.

When you make peace with this fact, then you can dress up modestly and not bother about what anyone is saying about your body. All you need to be confident is already within you; all that is left is just for you to explore your potentials. You are what more than you give yourself credit for.

Final Thoughts

This is an era of change. We are changing the narrative in the fashion industry and will no longer clothe ourselves in just anything that is churned out there. We have respect for our bodies and will clothe ourselves in all modesty. We are having a shift in perspective and are beginning to see ourselves as powerful women who do not need to prove anything with our bodies. This is the pledge I want you to join thousands of confident women out there in making today.

From what we have done in this book, I believe you have come to terms with the fact that modest fashion is not for Muslim women alone. It is for every woman who has respect for her body. People, especially men, respect you when they see that you have much to bring to the table and are not eager to show off your body like a very large percentage of women do. This is not to say that women who dress modestly are better than women who dress indecently. But remember, there is only one first impression and you really would not like to take chances.

As you are changing your wardrobe to accommodate modest fashion, you should also seize this opportunity to change some aspects of your character that are not befitting for an honorable woman. You are powerful and should be a role model for the younger generation. You are empowered to empower others. Be modest in your dealings with people and shun every form of pride or arrogance. The change you are undergoing should be holistic and affect all areas of your life because if you dress modestly but your character stinks, you may give a good first impression with your looks, but when a person comes closer to interact with you, they will experience some disappointment.

In this book, I have shown you some positive steps you could take to discover who you truly are and live your life unapologetically as a confident woman. Women empowerment begins from within you. It is the work you have done on your personality that will present you as a confident woman out there.

Now that we have come to the end of our interaction, I want you to start practising what you have learnt from this book. Change your attitude towards fashion; develop a personal style and work towards empowering yourself to be a confident woman.

If you have gotten used to some bad habits over the years, you can take your time and unlearn them in the same way you had learnt them. Everything you imagine you can do is possible only if you set your mind to it. Do not be discouraged in your journey of modest fashion if people around you do not understand at first and maybe make fun of you. A confident woman does not let external circumstances determine her reactions to situations. Dress modestly; go out there and rule the world.

Cheers!